I0883224

Barcelona Sketchbook

HOMAGE TO CATALAN ARCHITECTURE

LAURENCE KING

A Talisman Book for Laurence King

First published in 2018 by

Talisman Publishing Pte Ltd
talisman@apdsing.com
www.talismanpublishing.com

Laurence King Publishing Ltd
361–373 City Road
London EC1V 1LR
United Kingdom
email: enquiries@laurenceking.com
www.laurenceking.com

A catalogue record for this book is available from the British Library

ISBN: 9781786272195

Printed in Singapore

Editor Kim Inglis
Designer Norreha Sayuti
Design Assistant Nie Mingchu
Studio Manager Janice Ng
Publisher Ian Pringle

The pretty pink facade of the Parliament de Catalunya belies its original purpose of military arsenal of the fortified citadel that once stood on this site. The arsenal was designed by the military engineer George Prosper Van Verboom who built the nearby Garrison church. In 1932 it was approved as the seat of the Catalan Parliament but Civil War and Dictatorship intervened and it only reopened in 1980.

Barcelona Sketchbook

HOMAGE TO CATALAN ARCHITECTURE

Paintings by Graham Byfield
Written by Marcus Binney

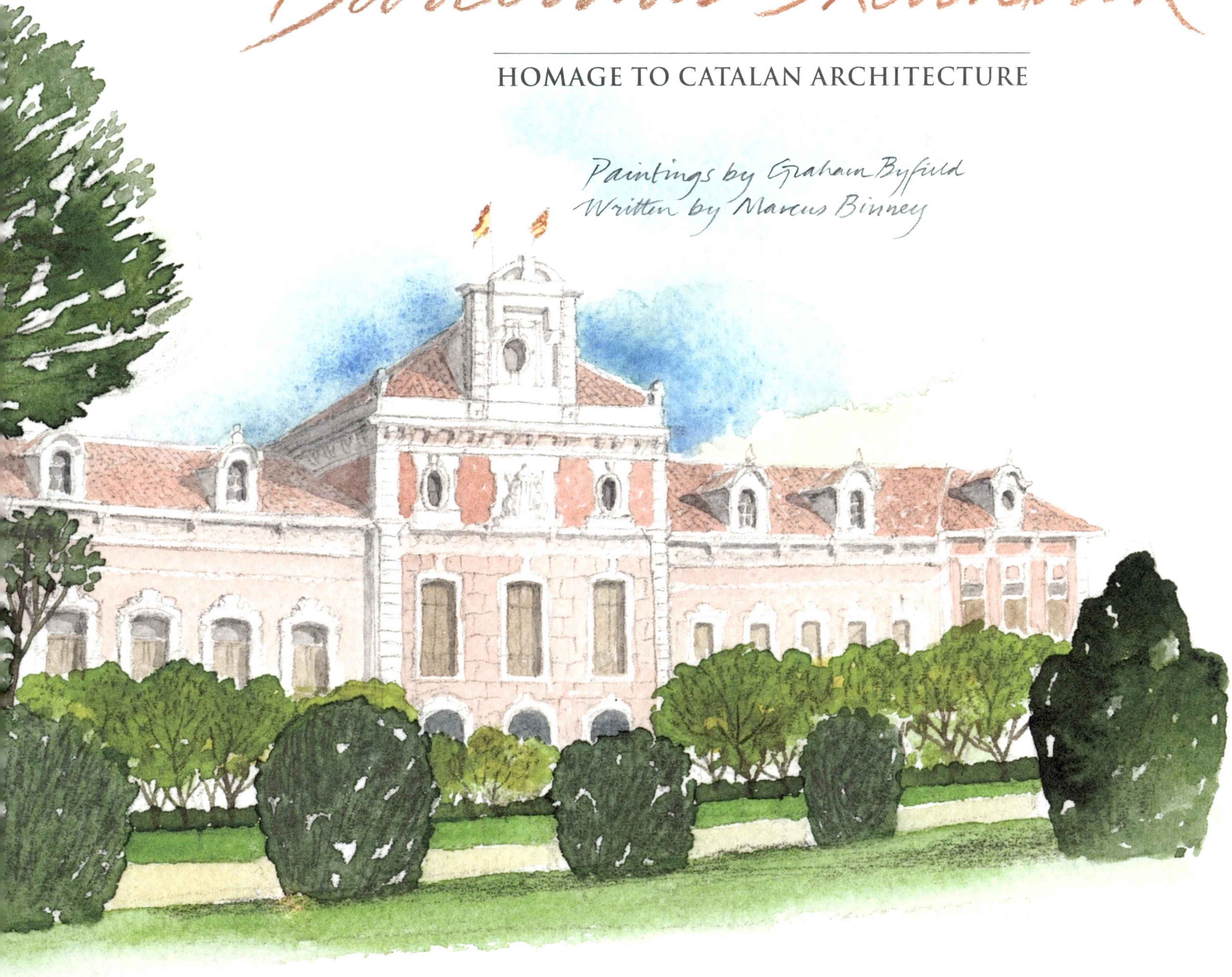

Contents

Gaudí's Bellesguard, built in 1900-09, draws inspiration from a medieval castle that stood on the site. Gaudí created his own distinctive vocabulary of Gothic detail with pointed windows, machicoulis and battlements and a strongly defensive entrance.

Exploring Barcelona

Exotic, extravagant, exhilarating … the architecture of Barcelona is in a class of its own. Today the city is renowned above all for Art Nouveau, or *Modernisme* as the Catalans call it, embracing the whole spectrum of later 19th- and early 20th-century styles.

Nonetheless, it is a story that begins with what remains of a Roman wall with 74 towers within a medieval city. Here, there are medieval palaces with courtyards as impressive as many in Venice — three occupied by the Picasso Museum. Parish churches vie with the cathedral in the splendour of their vaults and great rose windows. With patience and a good map, one can also discover quite a wealth of Renaissance, Baroque and Neo-Classical architecture along with the explosion of creativity that followed in the 19th century as Barcelona rose to become the most prosperous industrial and commercial city in Spain. Since the death of Franco in 1975, Barcelona has once again become a fulcrum of avant-garde creative architecture, earning a name as a style-setting city, celebrated in design and travel magazines the world over.

Equally exciting is the 'return to glory' evident in the revival, and repair, of its historic architecture. Barcelona does not rest on its laurels. Every year more buildings open their doors to the public, including opulent family houses by Gaudí and his contemporaries. The completion of Gaudí's Sagrada Família and the current restoration of the vast Art Nouveau former Hospital de la Santa Creu i Sant Pau rank among the greatest projects of their kind in the world.

A passionate individuality is stamped on everything, beginning with the Catalan language and architecture, and part of the joy of Barcelona is that so much of it can be explored, like Venice, on foot. The city's most famous street, La Rambla, is an all-absorbing two- or three-hour stroll, with stops for cakes and aperitifs. When needed, buses, metro and taxis speed you to more distant destinations. For cycling enthusiasts, a mountain cycle way already provides dramatic views and will soon ring the city.

When the Royal Institute of British Architects broke with 150 years of tradition and gave its annual gold medal not to an architect, but to the city

Torre Agbar
This torpedo-shaped tower by the French architect Jean Nouvel has a colourful pixelated surface echoing the tilework of Art Nouveau buildings. In the foreground is the Museum of Design.

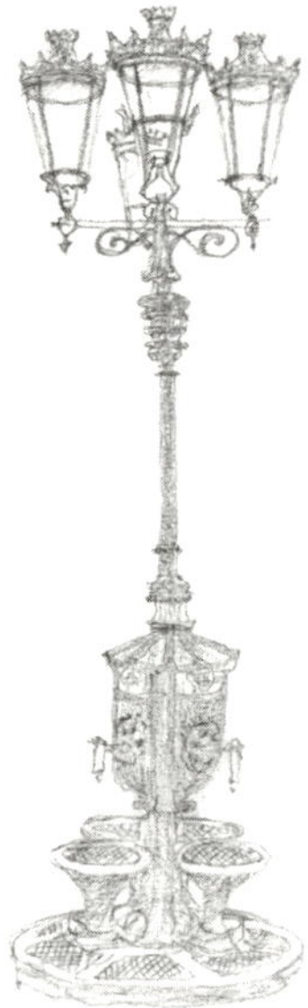

Intricate ironwork lamps are a delightful feature of Barcelona's tree-lined streets.

of Barcelona, I asked Peter Hodgkinson, a British architect who established with Ricardo Bofill a renowned studio in Barcelona, what the special appeal of Barcelona was. He replied: "I came here 33 years ago and fell in love with the country, the food and the wine.

"Architects are much freer here. There's no dominant international style. Better still, architecture is not so developer-led. As designers, we have a much greater control of projects from design to completion.

"We begin at ten in the morning and continue until ten at night, breaking for two hours at lunch. Dinner begins at 11 and the nightlife at one o'clock. There's snow in the Pyrenees, miles of glorious beaches, and I have a farm in the hills with a vineyard."

Few architects of any age have left a more sparkling legacy to their home city than Antoni Gaudí. Standing in front of Casa Batlló, watching dozens of visitors snapping photographs and gazing in admiration, you might think a royal princess or a film star had stepped out on the balcony. But here it is architecture that is playing the starring role. It enthralls by its romance, colour and imaginative detail. More than a century after it was completed, Casa Batlló retains its originality and novelty. It is Modernism, but of a non-conforming kind.

Gaudí, nonetheless, was designing in a city where buildings — great and small — have long had a special exuberance, an element of supercharging beyond other cities. Spain has many wonderfully preserved and dignified

Plaça de Catalunya. Considered both the city centre and where the old city meets the 19th-century Eixample, this busy plaza is known for its statues and fountains. Some of the city's most important streets meet here including the Passeig de Gràcia and the Rambla. A great place for visitors to start exploring the city.

historic city centres, but Barcelona has a cornucopia of architectural riches rivaled only by the greatest capital cities.

Its architectural splendours are the product of Catalan architects and craftsmen, born, bred and trained in Barcelona and its surroundings. By contrast, in the British cities that grew prodigiously during the Industrial Revolution — Liverpool, Glasgow and Manchester — the most handsome and exciting buildings were designed by both national and local architects.

Barcelona was the more remarkable in having superb architectural schools and technical colleges in which many leading Catalan architects were teaching. This was a process that began in the mid 19th century as the Eixample was laid out and continued through until Civil War broke out in 1936.

With the arrival of democracy, a more international approach has flourished. Architects like Arata Isozaki from Japan, Jean Nouvel from France, Norman Foster and Richard Rogers from Britain, Herzog and de Meuron from Switzerland, and Frank Gehry from Los Angeles have received major commissions. Yet Catalan architects still continue in full vigour.

HISTORY

Barcelona's origins date back to the 1st century BC. In about 15 BC, under the rule of Augustus, the greatest of Roman Emperors, a *castrum*, or military camp, was formed on Mons Taber, a small hill near the present City Hall in the Plaça de Sant Jaume. Though it was eclipsed by its neighbour Tarragona, where a great Roman aqueduct survives today, the new city prospered thanks to a good harbour.

The Roman grid is evident in the Gothic Quarter where substantial sections of Roman wall are visible. The later

In 1922, American architect Frank Gehry installed his sculpture of a giant goldfish on the waterfront at the Olympic Marina. With the sun reflecting off its golden scales it looks as though it longs to jump into the Mediterranean.

Plaça de George Oswell in the Gothic District was named after the British writer who penned "Homage to Catalonia" in 1938. The book is a personal account of his experiences and observations in the Spanish Civil War.

history of Barcelona has been turbulent. Visigoths conquered the city in the early 5th century only to lose it to the advancing Arabs in the 8th. In 801 it was taken back by Louis, son of the Holy Roman Emperor Charlemagne. Nearly two centuries later, in 985, it was sacked by the army of the fearsome Almanzor who brought Muslim rule in Iberia to its greatest extent, in an invasion in which nearly half the population died or was enslaved.

Barcelona became dominant among the Catalan counties under the rule of Ramon Berenguer I, Count of Barcelona (1023–76). He promulgated one of the earliest written codes of Catalan law. Intriguingly, the Catalans are cited in an early 12th-century Pisan chronicle which describes the conquest of the island of Menorca by a joint force of Italians, Catalans and Occitans (southern French).

The counties that made up the Principality of Catalonia were gradually unified by the Counts of Barcelona, and in 1137 were united with the Kingdom of Aragon. The Catalans nonetheless remained distinct, with their own language and their own line of rulers, all rejoicing in unusually colourful names. First came Alfons the Troubadour (reigned 1164–96), followed by Peter I the Catholic, James I the Conqueror, Peter II the Great, Alphonse II the Liberal, James II the Fair (El Just), Alphonse II the Kind (El Benigne), Peter III the Ceremonious, John the Hunter and finally Martin the Humanist who died in 1410.

Under the Catalan kings Barcelona's political and commercial importance grew and the city expanded beyond its Roman walls developing around new parishes outside the walls. The long reign of James the Conqueror saw expansion into Languedoc, Valencia and the Balearic Islands, and a surge in maritime trade. His autobiographical manuscript *Book of Deeds* (*Llibre dels fets*) describes his part in the Reconquista of the Iberian Peninsula from Muslim rule. Peter the Great conquered Sicily and became its king in 1282. James the Fair was granted the Kingdom of Sardinia and Corsica. Martin brought peace to his dominions and he supported the Avignon Popes, the Aragonese Pope Benedict XIII who held the See throughout his reign.

Santa Caterina Market dating from 1848 has been dramatically transformed with a colourful wave roof by Catalan architects Enric Miralles and Benedetta Tagliabue.

A more peaceful era opened in 1469 with union of Aragon and Castile through marriage. Yet anarchy and rebellion continued to play a significant role. The Catalan Revolt of 1640–59 began when Catalan peasants rebelled against the quartering of Castilian troops in their homes. A Catalan Republic was proclaimed in January 1641, and this was followed by the Battle of Montjuïc when Spanish forces were defeated in their attempt to retake the city. Anarchy grew, posing a threat to the nobility and the Church who hastened to accept the protection of Louis XIII of France.

The Spanish only retook Barcelona in 1652, a full four years after the Peace of Westphalia had brought an end to fighting in the rest of Europe. Meanwhile, a great plague raged between 1650 and 1654, halving the city's population.

Prosperity returned in the later 17th century, but Catalonia was soon swept into the War of the Spanish Succession with France and Spain pitted against Britain and the Hapsburgs (Louis XIV's Grande Armée confronted the Duke of Marlborough and Prince Eugene of Savoy). During the Siege of Barcelona in 1705 an army led by the English Lord Peterborough seized Barcelona from the Bourbons. In turn the next year the Spanish, led by Philip V of Spain, laid siege, but the siege was abandoned when a large English fleet arrived with reinforcements.

Barcelona and all Catalonia remained in Allied hands until 1714. Despite the Peace of Utrecht that summer, the General Estates of Catalonia decided to fight on and the Bourbons embarked on a new siege, ironically led by the Catholic son of King James II of England, the Duke of Berwick, who had become one of Louis XIV's leading generals. The walls were breached on September 11 and, to avoid further loss of life, Berwick allowed the Allied troops to leave bearing their swords as a mark of respect for the defenders' courage.

The 18th century brought peace, until the French Revolution brought another destructive invasion in 1793. French armies surged into Catalonia, armed with new printed folio volumes of the antiquities and treasures of Catalonia which French Revolutionary troops used as a guide to pillage churches, monasteries and public buildings.

The 19th century saw Spain battered by the Carlist wars between the Royalists rallying to the cry of "God, Country and King" and the liberals and republicans who were strong in Catalonia. Nevertheless, Barcelona prospered through these troubled times thanks to rapid industrialization. Though its autonomy within Spain varied constantly, the Catalan language was the focal point of a literary and cultural revival known as the the Renaixença.

At this time, the Anarchists played a strong role and achieved the first eight-hour working day in Europe in 1919. However, the power of the Left was set back in 1925 by the dictatorship of Primo de Rivera. On his fall the Left gained further ground, but the struggle led inexorably to full scale Civil War from 1936–39. The crushing victory of the Fascist General Franco was a catastrophe for Catalonia — and the use of the Catalan language was banned and all forms of self-government terminated.

Nonetheless, the 1960s saw a tourist boom and industry revived with Spain's first mass car manufacturer SEAT established in Barcelona in 1949. Following Franco's death Barcelona burst back into life under a series of dynamic City Mayors, culminating in the Barcelona Olympics in 1992.

This galley is a superb reconstruction of the flagship of Don Juan of Austria, victor of the decisive Battle of Lepanto in 1571 against the Ottoman navy. Painted in the red and gold colours of Spain, it was completed in 1971 to mask the 400th anniversary of the great battle.

Soldiers in original military uniforms guard the old city walls.

Cases Rocamora
The beehive domes and rows of arched windows make these a counterpart of Madras Railway Station in India. They were completed in 1914 to the designs of Bonaventura & Joaquim Bassegoda and look over the main square, the Plaça de Catalunya.

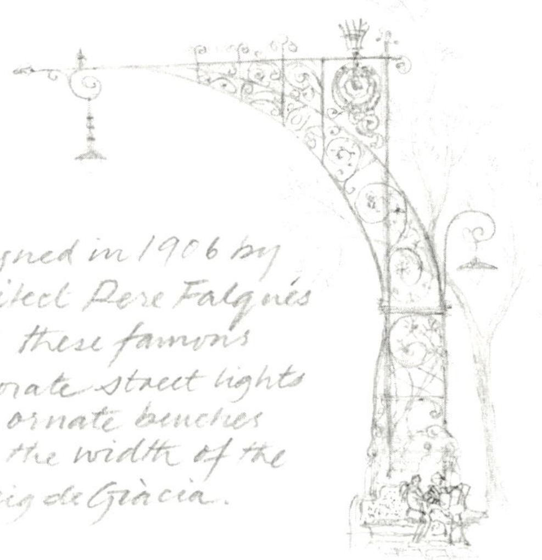

Designed in 1906 by architect Pere Falqués i Urpí these famous elaborate street lights and ornate benches span the width of the Passeig de Gràcia.

MEDIEVAL BARCELONA

Since Ancient Roman times great cities have been imbued with splendour by public buildings. In these Barcelona excels — palaces, churches, and a wealth of civic buildings: schools, colleges, hospitals, theatres, markets and port offices.

The Gothic Quarter, with its narrow streets, many closed to motor traffic except taxis and service vans, is a complete contrast to the rest of Barcelona. In the mid 19th century it was condemned as a slum (and again in the mid 20th). Yet poverty can be a great preserver and, thankfully, many old buildings survived with few modern intrusions during the damaging 1960s and '70s. Today, behind the austere stone facades, there are signs of investment — smart hotels and design shops alongside traditional food stores and family-run bars and restaurants.

The Gothic Quarter stands on the site of the old Roman *castrum*, hence the quasi grid plan and straight streets. But many of the alleys turn abrupt corners and it is easy to get lost, though not for long. Impressive sections of Roman wall appear in courtyards and piazzas — pointed out on discreet screens providing information for tourists. Roman masonry can be seen in the Plaça Nova and Carrer de la Palla.

Hidden behind the grand Classical facades of public buildings are a group of magnificent medieval halls. The 14th-century Hall of Transactions in La Llotja (the medieval Stock Exchange) is concealed within a dignified neo-Classical exterior. Here clustered colonettes carry arches that create a nave and aisles broader than many medieval churches.

The Drassanes Reials or Royal Shipyards are a series of lofty shipbuilding halls that produced the great galleys of the Aragonese fleet, one of the most powerful in the Western Mediterranean. Today they house a Maritime Museum with a full-size reconstruction of the flagship at the Battle of Lepanto where the powerful Ottoman navy was resoundingly defeated.

Some cities have constantly rebuilt their centres. Barcelona, like Prague, Havana and Vienna, has grown by a series of extensions. To the medieval Barri Gótic were added elements of Renaissance town planning. La Rambla, lined with monasteries and palaces, became a focus of city life; and the nearby Plaça Reial was laid out by Francesc Molina in the late 1830s.

EIXAMPLE

In the 19th century came the hugely ambitious Eixample. This is more complex than the famous gridiron plan of New York's Manhattan. The Eixample is one of Europe's boldest and most extensive essays in 19th-century town planning, to be compared with Baron Haussmann's reshaping of Paris and the Ringstrasse in Vienna. It is the creation of a visionary town planner, Ildefons Cerdà i Sunyer, whose motivation was to provide an abundance of light and fresh air in contrast to the narrow streets of the Gothic Quarter.

As the old city walls were demolished, the city council held a competition for the masterplan of a new extension or Ensanche. The city fathers chose the project of a local man, Antoni Rovira i Tras, with straight streets fanning out from the Plaça de Catalunya. Suddenly, the order came from Madrid for Cerdà's plan to be adopted instead (possibly because his consistently broad straight streets made for easier troop movements in a long rebellious city). The city fathers felt that Cerdà had ignored the old city (thankfully for posterity he left it intact), but his plan did address the problems of the Raval, a working-class quarter with cramped accommodation and an alarming death rate. There he found that a diet of bread and potatoes with the occasional sardine was all many families could afford.

Cerdà had trained as a civil engineer in Madrid before settling in Barcelona in 1848. Following the death of his brothers he inherited the family fortune and devoted himself to town planning, creating his own highly accurate survey plans of Barcelona. In the process of his great endeavour, he lost his fortune, never having been paid for his masterpiece.

His visionary solution was a grid plan consisting of 520 parallel blocks or *manzanas*. Cerdà called them *illes* (Catalan for 'islands'), each a square with the corners cut away. This created a distinctive pattern of octagonal city blocks and diamond-shaped intersections. The chamfers had a purpose — the dimensions precisely reflect the turning curve of a horse-drawn tram.

Cerdà's idea was that each block would be built up on only two sides with shared gardens in between, visible to the street on the other two sides. Heights were to be restricted to 16 metres ensuring maximum sun and light. Instead, market forces took over progressively filling most blocks with ever bulkier buildings.

Just as Manhattan's strict grid plan is broken by Broadway, so the Eixample is cut across by the Avinguda Diagonal providing a broad fast link across the city punctuated at

As St George is the patron saint of the former Crown of Aragon, St George's Day is celebrated in many Spanish cities. Historically, sweethearts exchanged gifts – men gave women roses and women gave men books. Today, thousands of stands of roses and make-shift bookstalls are set up all over Barcelona and everyone joins in.

Casa Batlló facade.

Casa de les Punxes.

regular intervals by grand *rond-points* with statues and fountains. The Gran Via de les Corts Catalanes runs across the city parallel with the sea, while three distinctive avenues ascend the hill: the broad Passeig de Gràcia, lined with the most expensive property in the city and some of the finest Art Nouveau architecture; the more intimate Rambla de Catalunya nearby; and, further north, the tree-lined Passeig de Sant Joan with its fast-moving traffic.

Cerdà's plan was that each of the five districts in the Eixample would have its own market, schools, even hospitals. Progressively, his gardens were built over while car parks were excavated beneath. In recent decades a new organisation, Proeixample, backed by local banks, has been set up to buy back properties in the *manzanas* as opportunity arises. The aim is to create open spaces, pocket parks and patio gardens with shade-giving trees and benches and other facilities such as swimming pools. By 2001 eight blocks had been landscaped and another ten were planned. It is a slow process, but the welcome outcome is outdoor spaces for the elderly, as well as families and children.

Monotony is avoided in much of the Eixample by the sheer exuberance in the designs of facades. Look carefully and you will find constantly changing materials and colours. Carved stone vegetation bursts from doorways and windows; surging balconies relieve the flatness of facades; glazed bow windows stand like turrets at the corners of stylish apartment blocks; and parapets are given wild sculptural forms.

Fin-de-siècle Barcelona rivals Brussels in the number of surviving exotic mansions. The most famous group is the waspishly named Block of Discord, a collection that includes Gaudí's Casa Batlló built for a distinguished textile–producing family at the top end. Next to it is Casa Amatller, built by the architect Josep Puig i Cadafalch in 1898–1900 for the chocolatier Antoni Amatller. Its *sgraffito* walls are like gold wrapping paper; medieval mullioned windows are enlivened by lively animal sculptures including, bizarrely, a carving of a rat operating a plate camera; and window shutters have trelliswork and quatrefoils. The wealth of inventive detail is inexhaustible.

At the far end of the Block of Discord is the Casa Lleó Morera. Designed by Lluís Domènech i Montaner, it was a collaboration with a group of artists working on the mosaics, stone carvings and ceramics. The *tempietto* topping the corner has been reinstated, a vital flourish to the design.

Round the corner, at Carrer d'Aragó 255, is the Fundació Antoni Tàpies, a handsome industrial design of 1880–85 brought alive by a wire sculpture evoking the movement of a handheld sparkler. It opened in its new incarnation in 2011.

Gaudí's Casa Milà, open to the public, is one of the great sights of Barcelona where visitors can ascend to the roof and enjoy Gaudí's sculptural form at close quarters. It was commissioned in 1906 by an innovative businessman Pere Milà i Camps and his wife Roser Segimon i Artells. The wave-like facades are encrusted with balconies that have the colour and form of seaweed washed up with the tides and the stonework appears worn smooth by the action of water.

Higher up the Passeig de Gràcia at No 113 is the Casa Bonaventura Ferrer of 1905–6 by Pere Falqués i Urpi. It is now a hotel with carved foliage bursting into leaf from the mouldings of windows and doors. A few dozen yards further on at No 132 is Casa Fuster, also a hotel, a powerful Art Nouveau design of 1908 by Lluís Domènech i Montaner. Its less vegetal, more blockish detail shows a further evolution of Art Nouveau only three years later.

To fully appreciate the extravagant richness of the architecture of this era, many other individual houses are worth seeking out. Palau Macaya at Passeig de Sant Joan 108 by Josep Puig i Cadafalch is in rich Flamboyant Gothic with Spanish colonial overtones; while Casa Comalat at Avinguda Diagonal 442 is a riotous design of 1909–11 by the architect Salvador Valeri i Pupurull. Its exuberant wooden balconies and brightly coloured mosaic ornament are as rich as the embroidery on a peasant costume.

The 1904 Palau del Baró de Quadras at Avinguda Diagonal 373 by Josep Puig i Cadafalch has a first-floor bay window as intricately sculpted as a set of cathedral choir stalls. And at Gran Via 491 the 1901 Casa Golferichs by Joan Rubió i Bellver has crazy paving stonework; trefoil topped pointed windows; oversailing roofs like Ottoman houses on the Bosphorus; and a first-floor bay window encrusted with vivid green seaweed-like foliage. A few blocks further on, at Calle Llançà 20, one finds a huge arched gable with a mosaic evoking a giant butterfly. This is Casa Fajol, a design by Josep Graner i Prat dating from 1912.

Known as the House of the Butterfly from its colourful gable, the Casa Fajol of 1912 is by Josep Graner i Prat. The wings nonetheless could be mistaken for fishes.

Palau Montaner Evoking the architecture of Renaissance palaces, this opulent 1889 mansion by the architect Josep Domènech i Estapà has oversailing eaves and an elaborate pictorial freize.

Whitewashed houses, window grills, pot plants and cobbled streets evoke a typical Andalucian village in the Poble Espanyol. This is a survival of the 1929 World Exhibition with streets and houses lovingly designed to evoke the character and architecture of Spain's proud provinces.

On the corner of Carrers del Bruc and de València, the 1916 Conservatori Municipal de Música by Antoni de Falguera i Sivilla has neo-Gothic twin turrets. And one of the most opulent of Barcelona's mansions is the Palau Montaner at Calle de Majorca 278. Designed in 1889 by the architect Josep Domènech i Estapà, it is now the Delegacion del Gobierno Español with flags flying from the main balcony. It has the monumental proportions of a 16th-century Florentine palace with richly carved balustrades and over-sailing eaves. These protect an elaborate pictorial treatment of half naked Bacchanalian figures on a wine red background of tiles and mosaics. As the entrance doors open, there are glimpses of an opulent grand staircase and an abundance of bronze ornaments and light within.

Just across the street at Carrer Mallorca 283 is the Palau Casades, seat of the College of Advocates of Barcelona. Built to the designs of the architect Antoni Serra i Pujals in 1883–86, this has a handsome Classical front shaded by palms with a roof balustrade crowned with urns and statues in the manner of an Italian Baroque *palazzo*.

ROMANCE OF THE PAST

The breathless novelties of Art Nouveau were followed after World War I by a new love affair with the past, sparked by a subtle Romanticism. The fascinating results are to be found in the Gothic Quarter. They went beyond the careful and scholarly repair of older buildings and involved the addition of new features and enrichments to enliven plain masonry and also to heal the wounds on maltreated facades.

The recent discovery that what appears to be authentic medieval work is in fact the creation of the 1920s has brought accusations that a systematic attempt was being made to produce deceptive fakes under the banner of promoting tourism. Judgment should rest on whether the new work is done with conviction and a careful attention to detail, craftsmanship and materials.

The most delightful of these insertions is the charming Bishop's Bridge, a stone bridge crossing the Carrer del Bisbe linking the cathedral and the Bishop's Palace. It is finely carved with filigree ornament in Flamboyant style. Completed in 1928 to the designs of Joan Rubió y Bellver, it is an intriguing parallel to the similar Gothic Bridge at St John's College in

The monumental fountain in Plaça Espanya stands at the entrance to the 1929 Barcelona International Exhibition.

Cambridge, as it happens on the cover of the *Cambridge Sketchbook* in this series. That, too, is Gothic Revival — though 1820s, not 1920s. Both show that Revivalist architecture produces results that stand the test of time.

A much bigger essay in Gothic Revival was the completion of the unfinished front of the medieval Catedral de la Santa Creu i Santa Eulàlia. This was vastly enriched and given three pierced spires akin to those added to Cologne Cathedral in the 19th century. The work began in 1882 and continued till 1913 under the architects Josep Oriol Mestres and August Font i Carreras. The west front is seen to superb effect when afternoon sun shines through the spires, illuminating the carved stonework of the spires within as well as without.

Barcelona is exceptional at retaining the monumental buildings of the 1888 and 1929 Expositions held respectively in the Parc de la Ciutadella and the acropolis of Montjuïc. To these have been added the legacy of the 1992 Olympics.

An intriguing survival of the 1929 International Exposition is the Poble Espanyol (literally Spanish Town) on Montjuïc. Even though they may seem to smack of theme parks today, these recreated villages were a regular feature of international exhibitions and have historic interest. The Barcelona example is well preserved and open to the public. With plenty of craft shops and cafés, it has the passion and conviction of all Catalan architecture of this time. It was conceived by the leading architect Josep Puig i Cadafalch as a walled enclave containing streets and buildings typical of all the main regions in Spain. Two architects, an artist and a draughtsman set off in style, in a brand-new Hispano Suiza, on a research tour of 1,600 villages. The result may be a form of film set, but it is charming and full of surprises as you walk through twisting alleys, archways and steps looking at miniature palaces with balconies and coats-of-arms, pretty cottages, church doorways and bell towers.

WATERFRONT

The 1992 Olympics prompted a major transformation of Barcelona's seafront. Previously it was a rough rundown area of warehouses, sheds and railway sidings that cut off the city from the sparkling blue waters of the Mediterranean. Today it is something entirely different.

The liberation that came with the end of the Franco years brought a re-engagement with the sea. A dynamic series of city mayors transformed a 10km waterfront — an area as large as the Eixample — with promenades, parks, marinas, piers and beaches. First came Pasqual Maragall, elected mayor four times between 1983 and 1995, and Joan Clos. They worked principally with two architects Oriol Bohigas (who masterminded the Olympic Village in 1992) and Josep Acebillo.

A new Rambla del Mar, designed in 1994 by the architects Albert Viaplana and Helio Piñon, now connects the city's

Casa Arnús
This prominently sited Gothic Revival villa near the top of the Tibidabo Funicular Station was built in 1904 for a doctor Manuel Arnús i Fortuny by Enric Sagnier.

The 1888 column to Christopher Columbus was the first to contain a lift.

famous Rambla to Port Vell, the old port. And the starting point is the city's colossal monument to Christopher Columbus. Two other proud landmarks stand nearby: the Port Authority Building, painted a brilliant yellow and cream, designed in French fin-de-siècle style but gorgeously ornate; and next to it, the Aduana, a very Catalan version of the Imperialist style popular in Europe's leading cities in the years around 1900.

The eye is seized here by a striking wave colonnade that leads to the Maremagnum Shopping Centre; it is a wooden walkway that opens every hour to let boats through. Nearby is a tree-lined promenade leading to the district of Barceloneta, laid out on a triangular spit of land with a golden sandy beach on the far side. It was built to house families dislodged by the building of the Ciutadella fortress, now replaced by the park of the same name. The plan is that of a military encampment with buildings in the form of long narrow barrack-like blocks, not surprising as it was the work of a military engineer Juan Martín Cermeño. The original two-storey houses have been replaced by taller apartment blocks, but one survives as the local museum, the Casa de la Barceloneta of 1761.

NORTH OF CITY

North of the Diagonal are a series of architectural treasures which deserve an excursion. On the way to Parc Güell is one of Gaudí's early masterpieces — the Casa Vicens, superbly restored. A short distance away is Gaudí's Teresianes College and directly north another masterpiece, his Bellesguard essay in medieval fantasy.

Next door is the college of Sant Redemptor by Bernard Martorell (1922) with a church like a many-gabled wedding cake — a geometric version of Art Nouveau. Today it is the Abat Oliba CEU University. This is one of a series of grand college buildings in the Upper Town. Another is the Patronat Ribas, a parade of five gabled blocks to the south west, built as an orphanage by two public-spirited brothers. Designed by Enric Sagnier, it opened in 1930. Nearby is the CosmoCaixa Science Museum housed in a handsomely restored *Modernista* building of 1904–09 designed by Josep Domènech i Estapà. Festive rows of cog-like arches make it highly appropriate to its new use. Built as an asylum for the blind, it is now a huge attraction for children.

Further south is the beautiful Monastery of Pedralbes. With a cloister surrounded by a three-tier arcade, it now houses a collection of medieval art. The Royal Palace of Pedralbes, with an entrance on the Diagonal, is a 1920s royal residence transformed into a group of museums. Its handsomely planted landscape gardens are today a public park. Next door is another Gaudí jewel, the 1887 dragon gates and entrance pavilion to the stables of the Finca Güell, which lead into a garden that is open several days a week.

CHURCHES

Barcelona's medieval cathedral has a serious competitor: Gaudí's still incomplete Sagrada Família, also on the top list of sites for every visitor. There are also numerous other churches worth seeking out. You need to know that many were badly damaged on repeated occasions, notably during the brutal anti-clericalism of the Civil War.

The series of largely 14th-century medieval churches includes Santa Maria del Pi, Santa Àgata and Sants Just i Pastor, all with distinctive octagonal towers, but the jewel in the crown is Santa Maria del Mar. This is a soaring essay in vertiginous Gothic with the vaults of nave and aisles held aloft on soaring columns. It resembles the hall churches that are also found in the Hanseatic ports of the Baltic Sea, where the whole church is on view at you enter. Here the strong atmosphere comes from the bare exposed stonework and intense colour of the stained glass.

There is a handsome group of Renaissance and Baroque churches. On the Rambla is the distinctive diamond studwork of the Church of Our Lady of Bethlehem begun in 1680 after a fire destroyed the earlier church. Here the Jesuit architect Padre Tort worked with the sculptor Pau Diego de Lacarre.

The former Garrison Church of 1717–28 in the Parc de la Ciutadella has a Baroque front with characteristic giant Baroque scrolls fronting the side aisles. Designed by George Prosper Van Verboom, a Flemish military engineer in the service of Philip V, it was part of the star-shaped fort begun by Philip V after his victory over Barcelona in 1714. It is dedicated to Sant Felix Africanus.

The Basílica de la Mercè is another handsome Baroque church, this time built to the designs of Josep Mas i Dordal in 1765–75. The dome is faced in diamond-patterned tiles and topped by a bronze statue of the Madonna.

Ornate 19th-century churches number among the rediscovered wonders of European cities. In Barcelona a fine example is the Church of Sant Francesc de Sales on the broad Passeig de Sant Joan. This is full-bloodied Gothic Revival at its spikiest and the work of Joan Martorell, one of Gaudí's teachers. It was built on a lavish scale to serve a convent founded in 1874 by three Catalan sisters. Though sacked in the Civil War, it thrives again today and is a fashionable church for weddings.

Standing dramatically on the mountain above the city and dominating views from below is the Church of the Sacred Heart of Jesus, Barcelona's counterpart of the church of Montmartre. Both are examples of 19th-century Romanticism. The project was conceived by a Board of Catholic Knights fearful that the prominent site might be used for a casino or even a Protestant church. The crypt in full Art Nouveau style was built in 1903–11, but the church above took much longer to build, from 1915 to 1951, with completion of the towers taking a further ten years.

Still more ambitious is Gaudí's Sagrada Família, begun in 1882 and now racing to completion. Gaudí's original design envisaged 18 spires which will

Begun in 1141 by the order of the Holy Sepulchre, the peaceful, yet centrally located, Santa Anna church is a hidden gem. The 15th-century cloisters are particularly attractive and classical guitar concerts are often held in its courtyard.

Santa Teresa de L'Infant Jesus
The monumental stepped tower has a characteristic Expressionistic force above a broad cave like entrance of receding arches. It was completed in 1933 to the designs of Josep Domènech i Massana.

make it the tallest church in the world when complete. Even so, it will be just one foot lower than the summit of Montjuïc as Gaudi did not wish to rival his master's creations. The Basilica was the inspiration of a bookseller, Josep Maria Bocabella, founder of the Asociación Espiritual de Devotos de San José, which by 1878 had half a million members. He was inspired by a visit to the Italian pilgrimage church of Santa Maria in Loreto that contains the remains of Mary's house encased in a marble shrine designed by Bramante.

Gaudí designed the cathedral with three monumental entrances, dedicated to the Nativity, the Glory and the Passion. Each was to be crowned with four spires, representing the 12 apostles. Four others spires will represent the four Evangelists with a still taller one for the Virgin Mary and the tallest of all for Jesus himself surmounted by a giant cross.

Work halted as Civil War threatened and during the vicious bout of anti-clericalism Gaudí's workshop was ransacked. George Orwell in his classic eyewitness account of the Civil War called it 'one of the most hideous buildings in the world' but that is not the opinion of the citizens of Barcelona. Construction restarted in the 1950s and today the completion date is set for 2026, the centenary of Gaudí's death.

Twentieth-century churches number among the city's lesser known glories. The Sanctuary of Our Lady of Mount Carmel on the Avinguda Diagonal has a darkened interior in the Byzantine style with a shallow saucer dome echoing Santa Sofia in Istanbul. It dates from 1911–1929.

The Mare de Déu dels Àngels is an eye-catching modern church standing on the corner of Carrer Balmes on a prominent site. It has a conspicuous tower suggestive of a rocket and tall windows designed on a distinctive octagonal pattern with a feeling of Scandinavian Art Moderne. Designed by the Barcelona architect Josep Danés i Torras, it was completed in 1955, the year of his death.

My favorite find is Santa Teresa de l'Infant Jesús on Via Augusta. Designed by Josep Domènech i Mansana in 1932–40, the powerful rugged masonry is worthy of early 20th-century Chicago. The massive entrance portal, framed in receding arches, is set within an outer giant arch composed of alternating grey and buff stone. The latticework in the tall windows of the bell tower allows glimpses of sky beyond.

PARKS

Barcelona today is a vibrant example of successful high-density city living. Frenzied building has nonetheless gone hand in hand with the creation of gardens and parks. One of the pleasures of the city today is to seek out the best examples, beautiful not only for their lush Mediterranean planting and strong architectural design, but also for the breathtaking views many provide across the blue sea and green hills that embrace the city.

The oldest is the Laberint d'Horta, just north of the Ronda del General Mitre. This is an 18th-century garden in the grand manner laid out around the country villa of the Desvalls family. Today it is a much visited public park full of families and people enjoying walks through the extensive grounds. It was designed for the marquis Joan Antoni Desvalls who worked with the Italian architect Domenico Bagutti and the French garden designer Joseph Delvalet. The intriguing Moorish-style house is contained within the high walls of a circular courtyard with wings wrapping round. Immediately behind the house is a formal garden of clipped hedges and above it a maze or labyrinth formed of tall exquisitely clipped cypress hedges with statues of Diana and Cupid overlooked by an enchanting pavilion.

In the 19th century the park was extended in Romantic style, laid out in emulation of nature with winding walks, crags and tumbling streams and a waterfall. The designer was Elies Rogent i Amat. The Desvalls family gave the park to the city in 1967.

The Parc de la Ciutadella stands on the site of a large fortress built by the Bourbon kings of Spain to secure possession of Barcelona. The fortress was demolished in the 1870s and transformed into a park that served as the centrepiece for the 1888 Universal Exposition. The focal point is the Cascade dominated by a triumphal arch and an abundance of statuary emulating Rome's Trevi Fountain. It was designed by Josep Fontserè i Mestre.

The most famous by far of Barcelona's parks is Gaudí's Parc Güell. You usually needed a timed ticket but if you arrive and have no chance of entering there is a second best. The entrance ticket covers admission just to the central area housing the main Gaudí buildings and structure. Walk along the road and you will find a gate to the larger park behind which has Gaudí features, and includes magnificent walks and views.

Parc Güell was commissioned by Gaudí's great patron, Eusebi Güell, and like London's Regent's Park it was intended to be financed by the sale of residential plots. In London only half a dozen of the villas proposed by the architect John Nash were built. In Barcelona not a single plot sold and all that was built was a show house which, by serendipity, became Gaudí's home for 20 years in 1906. It is now the Casa-Museu Gaudí, with displays of extravagantly formed Gaudí furniture.

The site chosen was steep and rugged. Gaudi's entrance lodges step straight out of a children's fairytale — wildly undulating in form and with roofs suggestive of dragons. Steps lead to a hypostyle hall intended as the residents' market built with large Roman Doric columns. Above is a large terrace with a balustrade following the

Parc Miró
Joan Miró's sculpture of woman and bird is clad in colourful mosaic work. The former 1900 bullring in the background has now been converted into a very stylish shopping centre.

Barcelona's 1900 bullring was built in the bold Mudéjar style. With the decline of bullfighting it reopened in 2011 as a spectacular shopping centre designed by British architects Rogers Stirk Harbour + Partners. The facades have been preserved including this entrance with Moorish arch, topped by a new roof terrace and dome. Inside there are shops, restaurants and a Museum of Rock Music.

line of a whiplash and formed into a continuous bench seat. This is covered in continuous broken ceramics — Gaudí's favourite *trencadís* work.

The Laribal Gardens, near the Miró Foundation on the lower slopes of Montjuïc, were laid out by the famous French garden designer J C N Forestier, famous for his work in Havana. Taking their name from the lawyer Josep Laribal who donated the land on his death in 1908, the gardens contain numerous fountains and pools set into the natural contours of the hill. Immediately beside is one of the most beautiful of all the city's gardens, laid out in 1929 as part of the International Exposition. Called the Jardins del Teatre Grec, it can be approached down a dramatic descent of steps and fountains behind the Miró Foundation or more easily by steps up to a terrace near the archeological museum. It leads to a stepped open-air Greek theatre, but its most lovely feature is a formal garden of rectangular beds with pencil cypresses overlooked by terraces and pergolas. From here are ravishing views of the city and the romantically placed domes and towers of the 1929 Expo buildings on the hill.

The Parc de Joan Miró is one of a series of sculpture parks laid out on industrial sites, here with Miró's monumental sculpture 'Woman and Bird'. Nearby, the Parc de l'Espanya Industrial by the main Sants railway station was laid out in 1985 by the architects Luis Peña Ganchegui and Francesc Ruis. At one end is a large dragon with children's slides emerging dramatically through mouth and tail; elsewhere a series of 'lighthouses' evoke the chimneys of the factory than once stood here.

The Jardí Botànic on Montjuïc opened in 1999 with a focus on rare species. It was laid out by a team led by the architect Carlos Ferrater, with trees and shrubs from Mediterranean climes as well as southern Australia, South Africa, Chile, California and the Canary Islands.

Following the ban on bullfighting in Catalonia, Barcelona has dealt imaginatively with its bullrings. The Arenas de Barcelona, which opened in 1900, held its last bullfight in 1977. Under the direction of the British architect Richard Rogers, it has been transformed into a shopping centre. The great arena has become an indoor galleria ringed by tiers of shops and the new roof has become a giant belvedere terrace surrounded by restaurants with indoor and outdoor tables.

In complete contrast is the Monumental Bullring of 1914 at the opposite end of the Gran Via near the Plaça de les Glòries Catalanes. Designed in 1914 by the architect Domènec Sugrañes i Gra, this has a powerful presence thanks to its bare Mudéjar style brick and glistening blue and white beehive domes. Here time stands still as if the last bullfight was only yesterday. Visitors can walk in and around the arena in eerie stillness with ticket booths, doorways, staircases and ambulatories all unchanged.

LOOKING TO THE FUTURE

The thrill of exploring Barcelona, whether on a first trip or a return visit, is that there are always new sights to see. In recent years the 12 pavilions of the former Hospital de la Santa Creu i Sant Pau have begun to open, revealing the astonishing interior of the restored San Salvador Hall, and the lofty airiness of the ward blocks. Gaudí's Casa Vicens has become a museum, and there are guided tours of his Torre Bellesguard. In the famous Block of Discord, the neighbours of Gaudí's Casa Batlló can be visited, the Casa Amatller and the Casa Lleó Morera. These are town mansions to compare with any in Europe for sheer éclat and style. On the Diagonal, the Casa de les Punxes with its fairytale silhouette of turrets and spires is also opening its doors, while year on year Gaudí's Sagrada Família nears completion. In 2010 the nave roof was completed and it is now used as a place of worship.

Barcelona is a city that invests in its past as well as its future, with sparkling results that bring ever more visitors — and raise the bar from year to year.

Monumental Bullring

Dating from 1914, this is built in Moorish style with beehive domes and blue and white tilework. Since closure it has remained untouched and visitors can walk into the arena in eerie silence.

Catedral de la Santa Creu i Santa Eulàlia
The ornate filigree spires of the medieval cathedral create a spectacular silhouette above the giant portal with its receding arches. The spires were built in the late 19th century, inspired by the 15th century design on the sight.

The Gothic District

Though the fortified city walls were torn down in the 19th century, Barcelona's medieval core remains remarkably complete and unchanged. With its narrow alleys, the Barri Gótic as it is known in Catalan retains the character of a labyrinth, a place of mystery with an occasional frisson of danger.

At its heart is the city's medieval cathedral with magnificent pierced spires dominating a large piazza. Dedicated to Barcelona's co-patron saint Eulalia, it forms a complex of cloister, monastery and palace linked by an ornate covered bridge across the street, a conceit of the 1920s. The courtyard of oranges in the Palau de la Generalitat is one beautiful survival. Though the handsome Classical town hall gives no hint of the Gothic interiors within, the Saló del Tinell is a striking example.

Traditional fare is served to locals in family-run restaurants, while former warehouses and wine cellars have been taken over by up-and-coming chefs serving the latest fusion food. There are cocktail bars and designer clothes and one of the most famous makers of espadrilles in the Carrer d'Avinyó. Another discovery is the Picasso Museum, housed in a series of adjoining medieval palaces.

The Gothic Quarter retains a fine group of medieval Gothic churches, among them Santa Maria del Mar with soaring columns supporting aisles as tall as the central nave. Another glory is the Carrer de Montcada lined with medieval merchants' palaces laid out around paved courtyards with broad stone stairs ascending to the first floor.

The cathedral cloister, completed in 1448, has a pretty pond garden which is home to 13 white geese, marking the age of Saint Eulalia, to whom the cathedral is dedicated, when she was martyred by the Romans.

The Ayuntamiento or City Hall has a grand columned centrepiece and stands on Plaça de Sant Jaume, the site of the ancient Roman Forum, opposite the Palau de Generalitat de Catalunya. It was completed in 1847 to the designs of Josep Mas.

The broad stone arches of the Saló del Tinell carry the transverse wooden beams of the ceiling creating a vast column-free hall. It was built in 1350-70.

The enchanting bridge over Carrer del Bisbe in Flamboyant Gothic style actually dates from 1928. Designed by Joan Rubió i Bellver, it is a prize example of 20th-century Romanticism.

View of the Cathedral from the Plaça Ramón Berenguer.

Palau de la Generalitat de Catalunya. Presently the seat of the Government of Catalonia and the Presidency of the Generalitat, the building's handsome main facade was built in the Renaissance and faces the historic Plaça de Sant Jaume.

Palau de la Generalitat de Catalunya. Looking from a first-floor loggia into the courtyard of the orange trees. (Pati dels Tarongers).

The Basílica de la Mercè is a Baroque church built in 1765-75 to the designs of Josep Masi Dordal with a dome surmounted by a statue of the Virgin, who is one of Barcelona's patron saints.

The austere but imposing facade of the 14th-century church of Santa Maria del Pi is inset with a large rose window with rich tracery. This reflects the Spanish taste for pure smooth masonry set off by bursts of carved detail.

The Picasso Museum is housed in a medieval palace with an open courtyard and outdoor stair ascending to a colonnaded loggia with pointed arches.

Plaça Reial
The former royal palace, the Palau Reial Major, is overlooked by King Martin's watchtower with its five arched loggias.

The Palau de la Música Catalana is one of the most extravagantly ornate Art Nouveau landmarks in the city. Designed by Lluís Domènech i Montaner, it opened in 1908. The richly detailed facades combine superb sculpture and colourful ceramics.

Many concerts are held inside the highly decorative auditorium. It is dominated by a massive organ and features a skylight portraying the sun.

Tapas and drinks are served in the café, one of the most exotic Art Nouveau landmarks in the city. There are outdoor tables beneath the arcade and a still more exotic interior within.

Passeig del Born
Thanks to traffic calming measures, this former jousting ground is now a pleasant treelined square leading from the Mercat del Born to the Gothic Quarter. Tall narrow houses are a reminder of the original narrow medieval building plots.

With its distinctive twin towers Santa Maria del Mar dominates the small square, popular with both locals and tourists alike.

This famous café which opened in 1897 was intended as a Parisian style haunt for artists, hung with their paintings including a large canvas of Ramon Casas and Pere Romeu on a tandem. Young Picasso drank here.

Barcelona's imposing university was built in 1863-82 in a blend of Renaissance, Gothic and Romanesque styles opening onto a series of arcades, courtyards and beautiful gardens. The architect was Elies Rogent i Amat.

The Baroque church of Sant Felip Neri (1721-22), a frequent venue for classical concerts, faces the charming square of the same name. Sadly, the square is probably best known for a bombing during the Spanish Civil War that resulted in over 200 fatalities. The shrapnel damage is still visible on the facade.

Barcelona's famous Rambla is a mile long promenade leading to the sea with traffic confined to the sides. There is space for flower stalls, bookshops and cafés as well as numerous pavement artists.

The Rambla and the Raval

Many Spanish cities have a handsome formal Royal Square surrounded by well proportioned Classical buildings. Here is Barcelona's Plaça Reial seen from an above window.

The Rambla is one of the world's most admired city centre promenades. By contrast to the monumental grandeur of the Champs-Élysées in Paris, with its magnificent vista open from end to end, the Rambla is intimate and relaxed, unfolding as a constant series of delights as its trees and kiosks conceal what lies ahead. It is a feast of vibrant city life with human statues, fountains, flower sellers, outdoor cafés and news vendors selling an absorbing range of guides, maps and postcards.

Its route follows the line of a stream which carried heavy rains from the Collserola hills in spring and autumn and in 1440 was diverted to run outside the new city walls. Increasingly it became a venue for festivals, markets and sports. The word '*rambla*' comes from the Arab for 'sand'.

The Rambla starts from the Plaça de Catalunya, the swirling centre of the city. Traffic is immediately calmed, confined to a single lane on each side and moving slowly so it is easy to cross and explore nearby streets. While the central promenade is broad, the narrow pavements at the sides are lined with a series of ornate shopfronts retaining original lettering and decorative treatments.

Barcelona's vibrant atmosphere is ever-present along the Rambla, with a wander revealing many architectural pleasures: The House of Umbrellas is an 1883 façade adorned with pretty oriental parasols and a dragon lantern on the corner; the elegant 18th-century Palau de la Virreina built in the 1770s for a Viceroy of Peru by the architect Carles Grau merits a venture into the oval courtyard; the Church of our Lady of Bethlehem, begun in 1680 after a fire destroyed the earlier church, is a Baroque marvel. And for foodies, opening directly off the Rambla is the city's most famous fresh food market, packed with shoppers and a parade of temptingly displayed shellfish, Spanish hams, game, ceps and luscious ripe fruits.

A bit to the south is the Raval district, a maze of narrow streets and small squares built on a medieval pattern like the Gothic Quarter. It grew within an extension of the city walls started in 1377. Known for its nightlife, it still has an edgy character requiring extra caution. The long Rambla de Raval is luxuriantly planted at one end. At the other is a popular monument of a large black cat by the Colombian sculptor Fernando Botero.

Negotiations going on for a trip round the city in a modern trishaw.

One of the festive iron street lamps in the Plaça Reial. They are an early design by Gaudí.

The 1770s Palau de la Virreina on the Rambla is named after the wife of a Viceroy of Peru. It is the work of the architect and sculptor Carles Grau and is now used for exhibitions.

Diners enjoy the atmosphere of a restaurant situated in one of the colonnades lining the Plaça Reial.

Following a savage fire in 1994 the Liceu Opera House was rebuilt retaining the ornate 1862 front entrance with its tiers of grand arches.

Mercat del Born
This restored 1876 Market Hall now houses the results of a large archaeological dig revealing remains of the Roman and medieval city.

Detail of the Japanese-style dragon at the so-called "House of Umbrellas." The zinc umbrella below was an emblem of the shop that used to be on the ground floor.

Inlaid pavement mosaic designed by the Spanish artist Joan Miró was inaugurated in 1976 on the Plaça de la Boqueria. Note the parasols adorning the House of Umbrellas across the road.

Our Lady of Bethlehem Church.
Following a fire this Jesuit Church was rebuilt in Baroque style in 1680-1729 but became a parish church when the order was suppressed in 1767. Though the interior was destroyed in the Civil War, the richly carved entrance and distinctive diamond pattern stonework survive.

Canaletes Fountain
An ornate late 19th century fountain situated in La Rambla is crowned by a lamppost and is a popular meeting point thanks to the saying that anyone who drinks from it will return to Barcelona.

Street artist on the Rambla

The 2009 ELISAVA School of Design and Engineering, one of the few modern buildings on the Rambla, deftly takes the colouring and proportions from its 19th-century neighbour on the left.
Artists work nearby drawing portraits of visitors.

The Born market hall now houses the results of a large archaeological dig revealing remains of the Roman and medieval city.

The restored Mercat del Born (1876) is a former public market constructed with iron. It is an early example of Modernisme in Catalan architecture.

Purchased by the city in 1987 and now permanently standing at one end of Rambla del Raval, this massive playful cat sculpture is by Colombian sculptor Fernando Botero. Surrounded by outdoor cafés, it has become an affectionate symbol of Barcelona.

MACBA

Museu d'Art Contemporani de Barcelona
Intended as a strong statement of contemporary art in the Raval area of the old city, it stands like a gleaming spaceship overlooking a rather lifeless plaza. Bold abstract forms dominate but do not engage with the surroundings.

A game of giant chessmen is one of the daily sights in the courtyard of the old Hospital de la Santa Creu i Sant Pau, now a museum and cultural centre.

Shopfronts along the Rambla feature old signs with floral Art Nouveau detail, angular geometric lettering and decorative mosaics.

Pastas Alimenticias is a famous bakery on the Rambla and has stylish lettering and decorative mosaics. Bespoke shopfronts survive in considerable numbers in Barcelona.

This well preserved shopfront combines floral Art Nouveau detail with angular graphic geometric lettering.

Outdoor tables with the famous Art Nouveau front of the Café de l'Opera in the background.

Antoni Gaudí

Gaudí, more than any other architect in history, created his own distinctive style. Skilled with his hands and highly observant, he drew inspiration from a wide range of sources including nature and natural forms. The son of a family of coppersmiths, he learnt how sculptural shapes could be created with a hammer.

Gaudí began his career with a stern Catalan version of Gothic with arched entrances, pointed windows, battlements and *machicoulis*. Many of his early buildings are in brick set in complex patterns inspired by Mudéjar architecture.

Gaudí was also immersed in the Arts and Crafts movement with its passion for fine materials and craftsmanship and love of exotic forms and rich detailing. Increasingly, he acted as artist as much as architect, creating buildings as colourful as paintings with rich sculptural detail. Façades, rooflines and roofs undulate like waves; the ironwork of balconies evokes seaweed or face masks; window openings have columns suggestive of animal bones and knuckles.

Gaudí was astonishingly fertile and, in addition to his large surviving oeuvre, he providing numerous imaginative designs which were never built. All his surviving buildings are worth seeking out including those isolated in the upper town such as the Casa Vicens, recently cleaned, and the brooding Collegi de les Teresianes. The wave-fronted Casa Milà, once decried as 'La Pedrera' or the 'Stone Quarry', has been restored to glory by the Caixa de Catalunya savings bank after years of decline. The Parc Güell is famous for its *trencadís* work — jigsaw patterns of colourful broken ceramics — a favourite Gaudí technique.

His most famous work, the cathedral of the Sagrada Família, is now moving towards completion in 2026, the centenary of the architect's death. As Gaudí famously said, "My client is not in a hurry".

Casa Milà. The serpentine walls and balconies suggest a mermaid's palace under the waves. Everything is on a curve with balcony fronts suggestive of seaweed.

Stained glass windows on the Piano Nobile of the Casa Batlló complement the surging curves of doors and ceilings.
Gaudí's expressively shaped windows reflect the inspiration he drew from nature, both animal and vegetable.

A pavilion roof with unusual battlements, finial and spirelet. Gaudí reshaped architectural features in a wholly personal manner.

This colourful front of fragmented tiles has a glazed roof like a dragon's back. The upper balconies are shaped like festive face masks while the first floor window surrounds echo the shape of animal bones.

Segrada Familia. The towers soar far above the trees below making this one of the tallest cathedrals ever built.

Gaudí's Passion Entrance with slanting columns can be seen through the trees in the park. The tops of the towers can be reached by a lift. The entrance was finished and designed by the Catalan artist Josep Maria Subisachs.

Segrada Familia is Gaudí's masterpiece. The four towers with the Nativatat entrance sketched in pencil from the inside area between the eight towers showing the Rose Window.

The interior of Segrada Familia is noless flamboyant than its exterior. Graham Byfield's sketch shows the rose window and its spectacular height; the cathedral plan is that of a Latin cross with five aisles.

A 1·8m-tall bronze of Gaudí, sculpted by Joaquim Camps in 1999, was blessed by a priest in front of the Segrada Familia before being relocated elsewhere in the city.

Bellesguard
Built between 1900-09 Gaudí preserved the spirit of the medieval ruins on the site in this spirited essay in the castle style. Note the exaggerated height of the tall Gothic window and the continuous bands of deep set arcaded windows on the top floor.

Palau Güell
Begun in 1885 for Gaudí's greatest patron Eusebi Güell this was intended as a distinctive statement of Catalan culture coinciding with the 1888 Universal Exhibition. It combines austerity with very rich detailing, notably ironwork of the twin entrances with parabolic arches.

Casa Vicens, commissioned in 1877, represents the earlier geometric phase in Gaudí's work. The client Manuel Vicens i Montaner was the owner of a brick and tile factory and could have hardly imagined a more georgeous display of his wares. The facades form a crescendo with richest motifs gathered at the top.

Collegi de les Teresianes

Dating from 1889, this striking early work of Gaudí still flourishes as a school. It is designed in a distinctly angular style with architectural enrichment concentrated at the top.

Casa Calvet on Carrer de Casp 48, was built to Gaudí's designs in 1899-1906. Though more restrained than other Gaudí works, his love of surging curves is manifest in the balconies and gables.

Looking down on the twin entrance of the Parc Güell. This is a fairy tale creation, full of exotic forms and glowing colour. The backs of the seats made up of fragments of glazed tiles was a favourite Gaudí technique known as Trencadís.

Close-up detail of Parc Güell entrance buildings.

The Dragon in Parc Güell is covered with ceramic fragments and stands at the top of the steps leading up to the Gran Plaça and designed by Gaudí.

The Port

With the arrival of democracy, the city's seafront changed from an industrial wasteland to a new world of waterfront promenades, marinas and revived dock basins. More recently, a new promenade, extending from the Drassanes Reials, a remarkable example of secular Gothic architecture, leads to the Port Vell. Opposite is the fin-de-siècle Imperial Aduana, a Customs House built on the scale of Buckingham Palace in London. Behind it, the festive Port Authority Building might be a casino on the seafront of Deauville or Cannes. The neighbouring Rond Point contains the Columbus Monument, an ornate column built for the fervently nationalist 1888 Universal Exhibition. It was the first such column to be installed with a lift and is topped with a costumed figure of the great discoverer pointing out to sea.

Further on, the Moll de Bosch i Alsina provides a leafy walk above the traffic racing furiously below. The Restaurant 7 Portes, sitting under the colonnade of the Pla de Palau since 1836, is the oldest in the city, grandly traditional for food, service and décor. The walk then sweeps out towards Barceloneta, first opening on to a large marina dominated by restored 19th-century warehouses which now house the Palau de Mar and Museum of the History of Catalunya. In front are inviting open-air cafés and restaurants.

Barceloneta is a planned village on a triangular spit of land with a golden sandy beach on the far side. It was intended to house families dislodged by the building of the Ciutadella fortress later replaced by the park of the same name. It is laid out like a military encampment with buildings in the form of long narrow barrack-like blocks, not surprising as it was the work of a military engineer, Juan Martín Cermeño. The original two-storey houses have been replaced by much taller apartment blocks, but one survives as the local museum, the Casa de la Barceloneta, in a house of 1761.

On the far left. A statue of Columbus pointing to the New World.

Aduana

The imposing Aduana or customs building of 1902 by Ensic Sagnieri Villavecchia, situated in the original port area, has a roof adorned in sculpture. On the left of the painting are the medieval shipbuilding halls, the Drassanes Reials.

The Port of Barcelona building is designed in a festive French fin-de-siècle style with a lively silhouette enriched by statuary and balconies atop the roofs of the corner towers.

Panorama of the port with the Columbus Column on the left. The Port Authority Building of 1903 is behind the trees. On the right the wave-topped colonnades lead to the Aquarium and the Maremagnum Shopping Centre.

Palau del Mar

A handsome range of late 19th-century warehouses, the Palau del Mar is now home to the Museum of the History of Catalunya. A tall graceful arcade ennobles the building while outdoor restaurants and cafés, enlivened by umbrellas, enjoy a view of the marina.

Mercat de la Barceloneta
Designed in a Futuristic style by MIAS Architects in 2007 it is situated in the heart of the old part of Barceloneta. The roof lights and canopies look like moving parts under which there are cafés and restaurants.

Two strikingly modern buildings at the end of the Avinguda Diagonal. In the foreground is the brooding slab of Museu Blau, a museum of natural sciences completed for the 2004 Forum of Cultures. Behind is the elegant triangular Telefonica Tower of 2011 clad in white steel trellis work.

Hotel 'W.' This giant hotel with 473 bedrooms was designed by Catalan architect Ricardo Bofill and stands on the Barceloneta boardwalk with spectacular sea views. Rising 26 storeys with an open air infinity pool at the top it echoes the form of a giant blue sail.

A 10-m high sculpture by Rebecca Horn of 1992 called the "Wounded Shooting Star" is a popular landmark on Barceloneta beach. Its inspiration came from the old sea front bars and restaurants that used to line the coast.

Port Vell is the old fishing port situated in Barceloneta. Compared with the modern port, things have not changed and it still has a wonderful old-fashioned atmosphere.

Built with a social purpose, this intriguing building fills the end of one of the typical narrow street blocks in Barceloneta. It was completed about 1917 to the designs of the architect Francesc Guàrdia i Vial with distinctive stepped brickwork to the cornice and window arches. The strong geometric character of the design heralds the arrival of Art Deco.

Barceloneta is the traditional fishing village where fishing boats unload their catch and fishermen still mend their nets and tend to their boats. It has a fine beach and the district is full of narrow streets built around 1900 with restaurants and bars offering excellent seafood.

Eixample and Modernism

Barcelona's Eixample is an essay in grand-scale city planning to compare with Baron Haussmann's Second Empire Paris. While Haussmann's grand avenues cut destructively through the historic fabric of Paris, the Eixample was laid out largely on new ground. It was an astonishingly bold concept extending to 520 city blocks bisected by roads ascending from the port up the slopes of Mont Tibidabo with inviting views of mountain greenery at the top.

It was laid out to the designs of Ildefons Cerdà i Sunyer, a Catalan urban planner. His vision was of a Garden City on the British model with tree-lined streets and leafy gardens in the centre of each block open on two sides so everyone, not just the residents of the new mansions and apartment blocks, could enjoy the sight of lush greenery. It was to be a democratic utopia, with no one neighbourhood grander than others. While the street widths remain entirely regular as planned, the Passeig de Gràcia and nearby streets rapidly became the most fashionable and expensive.

The creation of the Eixample coincided with the great flowering of Catalan architecture known as *Modernisme* that continued until the outbreak of Civil War in 1936. Modernism in other countries was intended to mark a complete break with the past banishing ornament and Revivalist styles. By contrast, in Catalunya, *Modernisme* embraces the full spectrum of architectural styles — Revivalist, Arts and Crafts, Art Nouveau, Art Deco as well as the Modern Movement. Though Gaudí's name rises above all others, the Barcelona School of Architecture produced a galaxy of talent, including numerous highly prolific designers working on private houses, apartment blocks and public buildings.

Situated on Passeig de Gràcia and known as the Block of Discord, this is the world's most inspired and gorgeous group of fin-de-siècle mansions with Gaudí's Casa Batlló on the right. The other fronts are in revivalist styles, but as inventive and delightful as any of their kind.

The stairway by Josep Puig i Cadafalch (1903) in the Palau del Baró de Quadras has a fine Art Nouveau mosaic floor.

These windows and balconies on an apartment block in the Carrer Balmes are an example of the rich and lively detailing of many later 19th-century facades in the Eixample.

The urban planner Ildefons Cerdà i Sunyer implemented a strict grid plan that included cutting off the corners of every building of every crossroads to enable the inclusion of green spaces within the Eixample's architectural environment.

Casa de les Punxes. Exuberant ironwork on an ornamental balcony.

The conspicuous Casa de les Punxes on the Avinguda Diagonal was built to the design of Josep Puig i Cadafalch in 1905 and evokes a vanished world of medieval chivalry with towers, spires and pointed gables, proving that architecture can look back and still be inventive and supremely picturesque.

The former Hospital de la Santa Creu i Sant Pau complex (1901-30) is the masterpiece of Lluís Domènech i Montaner. The entrance block is set unusually at the corner of the site with elaborate gate piers complementing the soaring spire behind.

In the main hospital building, marble columns with richly carved capitals, shallow pointed arches, brilliant pink saucer domes and coats-of-arms frame a view of the staircase leading to still richer halls above.

Casa Comalat
An unusual facade with brightly coloured bay windows on four floors all varying in design.
In 1909-11 it was designed by the architect Salvador Valeri i Pupurull.

The hospital wards and departments are designed as a series of free-standing pavilions set in gardens and connected by underground tunnels. The architect lavished attention on the detail of every pavilion with balconies, tempietto and dome ringed by ornamental torchères.

Lining the Gran Via are a multitude of apartment blocks with wildly exuberant rooflines fusing Baroque and Art Nouveau features.

Fundació Antoni Tàpies

This handsome brick and iron publishing house of 1881 by Lluís Domènech i Montaner was transformed into a gallery of modern art by Catalan artist Antoni Tàpies and contains a collection of his work. It opened in 1990 with a dramatic wire sculpture on the roof.

A picturesque essay in Spanish Renaissance style by Antoni de Falguera i Sivilla, the Municipal Music Conservatory dates from 1916-27.

Palau del Baró de Quadras
A rich Gothic Revival fantasy at 373 Avinguda Diagonal designed for Baron de Quadras by Josep Puig i Cadafalch in 1903. The richly sculpted oriel window fills the first floor merging with the balcony above.

Casa Golferichs
This gloriously exotic corner house in the Gran Via has bold overhanging gables and a projecting corner window in Gothic style matching the numerous richly carved groups of pointed windows. It was completed in 1901 to the design of Joan Rubió i Belver.

Montjuïc

Montjuïc is Barcelona's Acropolis, a massive outcrop of rock with beautiful views of both the city below and the sea beyond. Despite extensive building it retains its green mantle of trees and vegetation, all the more appealing in scorching summer sun. All this is thanks to good city planning. It could easily have been overrun by random speculative building of apartment blocks, but instead has largely been reserved for buildings with a public purpose and for landscaping and gardens.

Guarding the seaward side is a characteristic 17th-century star fortress with dry moat. In 1929–30 came the International Exposition that, despite the Wall Street Crash, proved an impressive success. The centerpiece is the monumental Palau Nacional, adorned with domes and towers romantically silhouetted against the sky. The exhibition buildings are a celebration of Spanish Renaissance style combining elements of palace, cathedral and monastery. The approach side is an exercise in the Grand Manner, satisfyingly symmetrical and approached by an ascent of staircases and fountains.

With the Expo came an Olympic-size stadium and numerous pavilions for industry and commerce as well as individual countries. Extensive gardens were created — among those especially worth a visit are the Laribal and Teatre Grec.

Later in the century, Montjuïc served as the site for the 1992 Olympic Games with a new covered stadium by the Japanese architect, Arata Isozaki.

The magnificent Palau Nacional was the centrepiece of Barcelona's famous 1929 International Exhibition and is superbly set at the top of a grand ceremonial ascent adorned by waterfalls. It was designed by Eugenio Cendoya and Enric Catà in Spanish Renaissance style with soaring domes and towers capped by cupolas. It now houses the National Art Museum of Catalunya.

The Archaeological Museum of 1929 is in a revived Florentine Renaissance Style. The front echoes the form of an ancient Roman triumphal arch with curving colonnades and an octagonal dome.

Matching in colour opposite the Archaeological Museum is the Teatre Lliure built also in 1929. It is designed in similar terracotta livery and has an octagonal dome & towers as well.

From the park behind, the silhouette of the Palau Nacional appears as a picturesque composition rising from the trees. It was the main site of the 1929 International Exhibition and since 1934 has been the home of the National Art Museum of Catalunya.

High up on Montjuïc the Joan Miró Museum is an essay in abstract form built to the designs of Josep Lluís Sert i López in 1975 and enlarged by Jaume Freixa in 1988.

The Olympic Stadium of Montjuïc was built in 1927 for the International Exhibition two years later, as well as Barcelona's bid for the 1936 Olympics, which were awarded to Berlin. Designed by the architect Pere Domènech i Roura, it was renovated in 1989 for the 1992 Olympics preserving the original facades with new grandstands within rising above the original walls.

The entrance to the stadium with steps for the runner to bring the Olympic flame into the stadium at the opening of the Games.

Palau Sant Jordi
Designed by the Japanese architect Arata Isozaki for the 1992 Olympics, this indoor sporting arena touches the ground lightly, hardly rising above the tree line. Today it is regularly used for concerts and other events.

Caixa Forum

This former textile factory by Josep Puig i Cadafalch in 1911 reopened as a museum in 2002. The new entrance was designed by the Japanese architect Arata Isozaki.

The Montjuïc Fort is protected by a broad dry moat planted with an ornamental garden parterre. The bridge leads to a classical gateway. Note the projecting turret known as a Bartizan.

The main square of the Poble Espanyol is modeled on the square at Riaza in the Province of Segovia. Surrounded by bars and restaurants, it is used for numerous events including concerts and markets.

The German Pavilion at the 1929 World Exposition ushered in a new era of elegant modern design, based on bold intersecting planes of walls and roof. An early masterpiece by Mies van der Rohe, it has been faithfully reconstructed using the same precious materials and achieving the original geometrical perfection.

Barcelona's Parks

Parks and gardens are one of the essentials of city living and Barcelona rejoices in an exceptional range of beautiful and unusual examples. Most famous is Gaudí's Parc Güell, so popular that it is often necessary to book tickets in advance. Around it extends a much larger public park, ascending the mountainside and thronged with walkers and joggers.

In the city below, the most important is the Parc de la Ciutadella, created on the site of a fortress built to subjugate the city and Catalunya and removed amidst much local rejoicing. It became the venue for the 1888 Universal Exposition. The centerpiece is a grand sculptural triumphal waterfall and cascade. The monumental entrance archway to the Expo survives as the entrance to the park and the Castell dels Tres Dragons, built by Lluís Domènech i Montaner as the Expo café-restaurant, also remains. It is held to be the first example of *Modernisme* architecture.

As the Fascist era ended, Barcelona's new independent mayors embarked on an ambitious programme for creating major parks often on disused industrial sites: A prime example is the Parc de l'Espanya Industrial with a line of tall columns — a cross between a factory chimney and a lighthouse. At the northwest corner is an iron dragon slide that enters a giant serpentine pool filled with pale turquoise water. Nearby is Parc de Joan Miró, planted with palms and pines and housing Miró's colourful sculpture 'Woman and Bird' covered in broken tile work inspired by Gaudí.

Other parks worthy of a visit are the Laberint d'Horta with an 18th-century maze and the modern Parc del Centre del Poblenou, created by the French architect Jean Nouvel in 2008.

The entrance to the stadium with steps for the runner to bring the Olympic flame into the stadium at the opening of the Games.

Near the entrance to Parc Güell these words on the enormous wall are made of ceramics and were designed by Gaudí.

'Crazy' Gaudí gates leading to the covered walk built in stone with leaning columns.

The house in which Gaudí lived for 20 years in Parc Güell is now a delightful small museum which exhibits a lot of Gaudí's furniture which he designed.

The 1920s Palau Reial de Pedralbes stands in a large park which is open to the public. From 1919 till 1931 it was the residence of the Spanish Royal Family when they visited the city – the property had been given by Eusebi Güell, Gaudí's patron, in thanks for the grant of the title of Count.

The transformation was carried out by the architects Eusebi Bona and Francesc Nebot. The entrance front with its forward curving wings overlooks a large pond surrounded by pots of geraniums. Today the Palace houses two Museums on ceramics and interior designs.

A Gaudí commission of 1887 was a perimeter wall and gates surrounding the so-called Güell Pavilions. He designed the main wrought iron gate in the shape of a dragon with glass eyes; the wall is in finely dressed masonry.

Parc de l'Espanya Industrial
This lively new park dating from 1985 was built on the site of a factory. The vanished chimneys find an echo in lighthouse structures which overlook the large fountain pool.

Parc Horta

The Laberint d'Horta high above the city is a large 18th-century formal garden laid out by the Italian architect Domenico Bagutti. The beautifully clipped maze above the villa is overlooked by a terrace with tempiettos in the corners.

Barceloneta Park.
The 60m Besòs watertower was built in 1882 to supply river water to the Eixample and later used to supply textile and engineering factories. Beside it is the ornate iron work of a former gas cylinder.

The Triumphal Arch which forms the entrance to the Parc de la Ciutadella was built as the main gate to the 1888 Barcelona World Fair. Designed by the architect Josep Vilaseca i Casanovas in Mudéjar style, it is adorned with friezes of figures portraying allegories of agriculture, industry and trade.

The Castle of the Three Dragons was designed by the architect Lluis Domènech i Montaner as a café restaurant for the 1888 World Fair. Though medieval in style with its towers, battlements and heraldic shields, it made extensive use of the materials associated with Modernism and Art Nouveau in the 1890s, notably terracotta and ceramics.

The grand fountain in Ciutadella Park has a waterfall issuing from a giant triumphal arch with frothing waters tumbling into a large pool below adorned with dragons.

The domes of the Palau de Justícia overlooking Ciutadella Park. Built in 1887-1908, it was designed by Josep Domènech i Estapà and Enric Sagnier i Villavecchia.

The gardens leading to the stepped open-air Greek theatre were laid out for the 1929 International Exposition. Their most lovely feature is a formal landscaping of rows of pencil cypresses overlooked by terraces and pergolas.

Tibidabo Heights

Whether by road or tram the ascent to Tibidabo Heights is exhilarating. Standing almost as dramatically above the city as Table Mountain does above Cape Town in South Africa, the Heights are not just a wonder of nature but are filled with exotic architectural interest.

The most obvious landmark, the church and minor basilica of Sagrat Cor, is sited so it looks out in all directions — inland as well as down to the city and the sparkling sea. It stands on a terrace with Art Nouveau grotto-like caves below and a casket-like Gothic church as highly wrought as an altar shrine. In 1936 the statue of Jesus crowning the church was an early victim of the anti-clericalism of the Civil War in Barcelona; a new statue was installed in 1950. At the same time, the hills had been denuded of trees by people in desperate need of firewood, though since, the mantle of trees has returned.

Tibidabo and the neighbouring village resort of Vallvidrera bristle with intriguing Art Nouveau houses. One is the Villa Tibidabo which retains its own gateway now painted a rich rust red. On the road ascending to the church is Villa Almirall, now available as a rental villa, and library beside.

North of the Avinguda Diagonal, though the distances are longer, there are more *Modernisme* landmarks to explore, as well as a grand series of colleges including the CaixaForum, now a Museum of Sciences intended to enthrall a younger audience.

Established in 1904, the Fabra Observatory was built on a site high above the city. Its main activity is the study of asteroids and comets.

The Church of the Sagrat Cor looms over Barcelona like the Sacré Coeur in Montmartre. It was built in two stages: first the cave-like crypt in 1903-11 in a strongly Art Nouveau style, and then the church seated on the terrace above like a shrine on an altar in pure neo-Gothic with a spiky silhouette of gables, spires and finials. Designed by Enric Sagnier and completed by his son in 1961.

This 1924 Library with a grand sculptural gable stands by a villa of the same name. Today it is let for events.

The Monastery of Pedralbes was founded by King James of Aragon in 1326 to house a community of Poor Clares, mostly members of noble families. The name derives from the white stone, pert as albes, from which it is built. The bell tower stands unusually by the main entrance in the flank, an invitation to prayer.

Villa Tibidabo
Ornamental iron garden gate belonging to a 1912 house designed by Albert Juan i Torner.

The cloister of the Monastery of Pedralbes unusually has three stories. Two graceful arcades of pointed arches are supported on slender stone columns with an open loggia above. Thanks to the temperate climate palms grow alongside cypresses and fir trees.

Vallvidrera

In this resort village on the heights above the city there are numerous houses in Art Nouveau style built as weekend and summer retreats. This group is opposite the Funicular station.

The original Blue Tram has been operating in conjunction with the Funicular to transport visitors to the top of Tibidabo since 1901.

La Rotonda enjoys a conspicuous site overlooking the small square on the crossing of the Via Augusta and the Passeig de Sant Gervasi. Completed in 1914 to the designs of Adolf Ruzi Casamitjana, it takes its name from a corner tower topped by a rich Gothic belvedere and wave parapet.

Patronat Ribas School is situated on the Ronda Enric Sagnier. Architectural patronage extended to building this handsome gabled orphanage in 1930 by Enric Sagnier with a central chapel. Today it is a school.

Gazetteer

This appendix lists a selection of buildings to visit. It includes many of the buildings illustrated and described in this book and is intended to lead the visitor to both well- and little-known buildings that intrigue and delight. Architects and dates of completion or construction are given where known, as well as street numbers.

GOTHIC DISTRICT

Temple of Augustus, Carrer Paradis, 10: 1st–2nd centuries AD. A cluster of fluted Corinthian columns survives.

Santa Maria del Mar, Plaça de Santa Maria, 1: 14th century. Soaring Gothic interior.

Santa Maria del Pi, Plaça del Pi. 1321–91. Large rose window and octagonal belltower.

Plaça del Rei: Large paved square surrounded by medieval buildings including the Palau Reial Major, the Palau del Lloctinent and the 16th-century Casa Padellàs, home of the history museum of Barcelona.

Santa Anna Church, Plaça Ramon Amadeu: Romanesque and Gothic. Hidden away behind the Plaça Catalunya and Av. del Portal de l'Àngel, it has the simplicity of a medieval country church with a beautiful shaded Gothic cloister.

Cathedral, Plaça de la Seu: Originally 13th–15th centuries, main front 1887–1913. Cathedral cloister 1382–1448. Majestic, atmospheric interior with beautiful cloister.

Basílica de la Mercè, Plaça de la Mercè: 1765–1775, Josep Mas i Dordal. Fine domed Baroque church crowned by a statue of the Virgin.

Bishop's Bridge, Carrer del Bisbe: 1928, Joan Rubio i Bellver. Enchanting Neo-Gothic bridge.

Els Quatre Gats, Carrer de Montsió, 3: 1897, Josep Puig i Cadafalch. Historic café restaurant, still flourishing.

Palau de la Música Catalana, Carrer del Palau de la Música, 4–6. 1905–08, Lluís Domènech i Montaner. One of the great Art Nouveau extravaganzas of Barcelona, inside and out.

Old Hospital de Santa Creu i Sant Pau, Carrer de l'Hospital, 56: 15th Century. Noble medieval and Renaissance courtyards now part of university; also houses the Biblioteca de Catalunya.

Casa de la Ciutat, Plaça Sant Jaume, 1: 1841, Josep Mas. Neo-Classical front on square with medieval Saló del Tinell within.

Palau de la Generalitat, Plaça Sant Jaume, 4. 1619. Gothic and Renaissance.

Museo Picasso, Carrer Montcada, 15–23: 2011, Jordi Garcés. Set in a group of handsome stone *palazzos* built around courtyards.

Mercat de Santa Caterina, Av. de Francesc Cambó, 16: 2004, Enric Miralles and Benedetta Tagliabue. 19th-century market transformed by dramatic modern wave roof.

Mercat del Born, Plaça Comercial, 12: 1876, Josep Fontsère and Josep Maria Cornet. Fine iron and glass market hall with floor excavated to reveal Roman and medieval remains beneath.

La Llotja, Passeig d'Isabel II, 1: Late 18th-century. Vaulted Gothic hall within.

Edifici Catalana de Gas i Electricitat, Av. del Portal de l'Àngel, 20–22: 1895, Josep Domènech i Estapà. Period piece with twin towers and electroliers.

THE RAMBLA AND THE RAVAL

Pavement Mosaic, Plaça de la Boqueria: 1976, by Joan Miró.

Gran Teatre del Liceu, La Rambla, 51–59: 1848, M Garriga i Roca. Opera house restored after a fire, reopened 1998.

Mercat de Sant Josep "La Boqueria", La Rambla, 91: 1860 and 1913–14. Magnificent foodhalls brimming with local produce.

Palau de la Virreina, La Rambla, 99: 1772–78. Viceregal mansion with inner courtyard.

Casa Bruno Cuadros, La Rambla, 82: Formerly the House of Umbrellas as the façade makes apparent.

Església de la Mare de Déu de Betlem (Church of our Lady of Bethlehem), *La* Rambla, 107: 1680–1732. Impressive Baroque church with diamond cut masonry.

Plaça Reial: Early 19th century. Built to the designs of Francesc Daniel Molina i Casamajó. An enclosed public square surrounded by graceful arcades.

Antiga Casa Figueras, La Rambla, 83: 1902, Antoni Ros i Güell. Elaborate Art Nouveau shopfont.

Museum of Contemporary Art, Plaça dels Àngels, 1: 1996. Richard Meier. A trumpet blast for White Modernism with a rather lifeless new square in front.

ANTONI GAUDÍ

Sagrada Família, Carrer de Mallorca, 401: 1883–present. Gaudí's masterpiece, unfinished at his death in 1926 but now racing to completion one hundred years later.

Finca Güell Pavilions, Av. de Pedralbes, 7: 1884–87. Enchanting entrance lodges with dragon gate.

Casa Vicens, Carre r Carolines, 22: 1883–88. Another spiky early work, and a highly personal version of Gothic.

Palau Güell, Carrer Nou de la Rambla, 3–5: 1886–90. A highly idiosyncratic early work, with powerful still Gothic detail.

Collegi de les Teresianes, Carrer de Ganduxer, 85: 1888–89. With the overpowering presence of a fortress, this school is rich in highly personalized Gaudí detail notably the steep triangular window heads.

Casa Calvet, Carrer de Casp, 48: 1899–1906. Gaudí's love of surging curves is manifest in the balconies and gables.

Parc Güell: 1900–1914. Landscape park, now public, with fantastic, colourful follies.

Casa Batlló, Passeig de Gràcia, 43: 1904–06. A flat façade transformed by Gaudí with dragon roof, balconies like face masks and sparkling colour.

Bellesguard, Carrer de Bellesguard, 16. 1900–09. Exuberant and eccentric, this is a supercharged Art Nouveau Gothic manor house.

Casa Milà ('La Pedrera'), Passeig de Gràcia, 92. 1906–10. Highly sculptural wave fronted apartment building.

PORT AND WATERFRONT (including PORT OLÍMPIC)

Duana del Port (Customs House), Passeig Josep Carner, 27: 1902, Enric Sagnier i Villavecchia. Magnificently ponderous neo-Baroque, proclaiming glories of Empire.

Old Port Authority Building, base of Rambla del Mar: 1907. A delightfully festive and rather French composition.

Palau de Mar, Plaça Pau Vila: 1890, Elies Rogent i Amat. General trade warehouses converted into a museum with open-air cafés in front.

Estació de França (França Railway Station), Av. Marquès de l' Argentera: 1929, Pedro Muguruza. Impressive concourse hall in Classical style with handsome train sheds.

Rambla del Mar and Maremagnum Shopping Centre: 1995, Albert Viaplana and Helio Piñón. Stylish promenade leading to new waterfront and aquarium.

Monument to Christopher Columbus, Plaça del Portal de la Pau: 1888, Gaietà Buigas i Monravà and Rafael Atché. Standing in a commanding position in the centre of a *rondpoint* and adorned with numerous statues.

Drassanes Reials (Royal Shipyards, now Maritime Museum), Av. de les Drassanes: 14th century. Immensely impressive covered medieval shipbuilding yard.

L'Estel Ferit sculpture, Passeig Marítim de la Barceloneta: 1992, Rebecca Horn. Charming folly in form of wobbly tower by beach.

Fish sculpture, Passeig Marítim de la Barceloneta: 1992, Frank Gehry. The master showman's contribution to the new waterfront.

Hotel Vela (Hotel W Barcelona), Plaça Rosa dels Vents, 1: 2009, Ricardo Bofill. Sail shaped and Barcelona's answer to Dubai.

BARCELONETA

Mercat de la Barceloneta, Plaça Poeta Bosca, 1: 2007, MIAS Architects. 19th-century iron and glass construction reinvented in a modern idiom.

La Fraternitat Barceloneta, Carrer del Comte de Santa Clara, 8–10: 1879 and 1918. Intriguing ornamental front to a corner building.

Torre de les Aigües, Parc de la Barceloneta: 1905, Josep Domènech i Estapà. Water tower of former gasworks in parkland setting.

Biblioteca de la Universitat Pompeu Fabra, Ramon Trias Fargas, 25–27: 1999, Lluis Clotet and Ignasi Paricio. Library intriguingly installed in former waterworks.

Torre Telefónica (Diagonal ZeroZero skyscraper), Plaça Ernest Lluch, 5: 2011, Enric Massip-Bosch. Elegant white lattice version of a Chicago-style triangular (flatiron) building.

Museu de les Ciències Naturals (Museu Blau), Parc del Fòrum: 2004, Herzog De Meuron. Massive slab structure elevated on columns in defiance of the sloping site.

Torre Agbar, Av. Diagonal, 209–211: 2005, Jean Nouvel. Shell shaped office tower with skin that changes colour by day and night, a brilliant modern take on Gaudí tile work.

CIUTADELLA PARK AREA

Parc de la Ciutadella fountain: 1882–88, Josep Fontserè i Mestre. Glorious sculptural fountain dominating the park.

Castell dels Tres Dragons, Passeig de Picasso. 1887–88, Lluís Domènech i Montaner. Built in fortress style as a café restaurant, it now houses collections of the national science museum.

Triumphal Arch, Passeig de Lluís Companys: 1888, Josep Vilaseca i Casanovas. Richly sculpted entrance arch to 1888 World Exposition crowned by trumpeting winged angels.

Parliament of Catalunya, Parc de la Ciutadella: Designed as an arsenal by George Prosper Verboom, it became the Catalan Parliament in 1980.

Sant Felix Africanus Garrison Church, Carrer de Sardenya 21: 1718, George Prosper Verboom. Handsome scrolled Baroque façade.

Palau de Justícia, overlooking Cuitadella Park. 1887–1908, Josep Domènech i Estapà and Enric Sagnier i Villavecchia. A building of monumental character.

EIXAMPLE AND MODERNISM

Casa Amatller, Passeig de Gràcia, 43: 1898–1900, Josep Puig i Cadafalch. Flemish Renaissance Revival mansion in the Block of Discord built for a chocolatier is as richly inventive as Art Nouveau itself.

Casa Lleo Morera, Passeig de Gràcia, 35: 1902–05, Lluís Domènech i Montaner. Set at the corner of the Block of Discord, it abounds with inventive Gothic detail.

Fundació Antoni Tàpies, Carrer d'Arago, 255. 1880–85, Lluís Domènech i Montaner. Converted as a gallery by Estudio Abalos Stenkiewicz in 1990. Extravagant wire sculpture on the roof of a former publishing house.

Palau del Baró de Quadras, Av. Diagonal, 373: 1903, Josep Puig i Cadafalch. Richly sculpted oriel window fills the first floor merging with the balcony above.

Casa Comalat, Av. Diagonal, 442: 1911, Salvador Valeri i Popurull. Brightly coloured bay windows, wave roof and tiles. Gaudiesque bone forms with a contrasting treatment on the street behind.

Cases Rocamora, Passeig de Gràcia, 6–14: 1914–17, Joaquim & Bonaventura Bassegoda. Conical corner turret and beehive domes on the Plaça de Catalunya.

Casa Fuster, Passeig de Gràcia, 132: 1908–11, Lluís Domènech i Montaner. Prominent corner site with inventive window treatment, now a hotel.

Circulo Ecuestre, Carrer de Balmes, 169 Bis: 1911, Joan Josep Heras Grimaldi. Lively Art Nouveau corner building.

Palau Macaya, Passeig de Sant Joan, 108: 1899–1901, Josep Puig i Cadafalch. Neo-Flamboyant Gothic encrusted with lively ornament.

Casa Golferichs, Gran Via, 491: 1901, Joan Rubió i Bellver. Full-on Art Nouveau, though the details are still Gothic.

Casa Bonaventura Ferrer, Passeig de Gràcia, 113: 1905–06, Pere Falgués i Urpí. Baroque inspired, now a hotel.

Casa de les Punxes, Av Diagonal, 420: 1905, Josep Puig i Cadafalch. Chivalric fantasy with delightful candlesnuffer turrets.

Casa Fajol, Calle Llança, 20: 1912, Josep Graner i Prat. Named for a butterfly on account of its colourful mosaic gable.

Conservatori Municipal de Música, Carrer del Bruc, 104–12: 1916–1928, Antoni de Falguera i Sivilla. One of the characteristic cutaway street corners of the Eixample with neo-Gothic twin turrets.

Palau Montaner, Calle de Mallorca, 278: 1889–93, Josep Domènech i Estapà and Lluís Domènech i Montaner. Very opulent palace in Revivalist style now Delegación del Gobierno.

Palau Casades, Carrer de Mallorca, 283: 1886, Antoni Serra i Pujals. Urbane town mansion, now Collegi d'Advocats.

Casa Sayrach, Av. Diagonal, 423–5: 1918, Manuel Sayrach i Carreras. Rounded corner of building surmounted by slender turret.

Toyo Ito Suites, Passeig de Gràcia, 83: 2009. Stylish modern ribbon façade by leading Japanese architect is a clever response to Art Nouveau.

Casa Enric Llorens, Carrer d'Enric Granados, 119: 1904–07, Josep Pérez i Terrassa. Distinctive corner building with first-floor bay windows.

Sant Francesc de Sales, Passeig de Sant Joan, 88: 1885, Joan Martorell i Montells. Spiky Gothic in terracotta and stone.

Mare de Déu dels Àngels, Carrer Balmes, 78: 1942–57, Josep Danés i Torras. Barcelona's answer to the Festival of Britain style in the 1950s, with rocket-shaped corner tower.

Santuari de la Mare de Déu del Carme, Av. Diagonal, 422: 1911–29. One of the few examples of the Neo-Byzantine style in Barcelona close by the Casa de les Punxes.

MONTJUÏC

Castell de Montjuïc, Carretera de Montjuïc: 17th-century spear bastioned fortress in commanding position above city and sea.

Casaramona Factory, now CaixaForum, Av. de Francesc Ferrer i Guàrdia, 6–8: 1910–13, Josep Puig i Cadafalch. Historic factory transformed into art gallery in 2002.

Palau Nacional, Parc de Montjuïc: 1927–29, Enric Català, Eugenio Cendoya and Pere Domènech i Roura. Immensely grand exhibition palace with towers and domes in vigorous Spanish Renaissance style, now National Art Museum of Catalunya.

Barcelona Pavilion: 1983–1986. Fastidious reconstruction of Mies van der Rohe's mesmerizingly beautiful Modern Movement masterpiece, originally built in 1929 for the World Exhibition.

Poble Espanyol, Av. de Francesc Ferrer i Guàrdia, 13: 1929. Recreated walled Spanish town with examples of regional historic buildings, both grand and humble.

Greek Theatre Garden, adjacent Laribal Gardens: 1929. Pergolas, terraces and parterres with ravishing views over the city.

Laribal Gardens, Passeig de Santa Madrona, 2: Impressive quarry garden of 19th-century origin with numerous steps and fountains.

Archaeology Museum of Catalonia, Passeig de Santa Madrona, 39: 1929. Designed as a Palace of Graphic Arts, it is one of a group of handsome pavilions surviving from the World Exhibition.

Teatre Lliure, Plaça de Margarida Xirgu, 1: 1929. Former Palace of Agriculture, now used for entertainments.

Fundació Joan Miró, Parc de Montjuïc: 1975. Designed by Josep Lluís Sert i López, then enlarged by Jaume Freixa in 1988. Distinctive shapes announce the great artist on show within.

Palau Sant Jordi, Passeig Olímpic, 5–7: 1990, Arata Isozaki. The distinctive pin cushion roof is designed to bed the indoor sporting arena in the landscape.

Olympic Stadium: 1920s. Huge Roman-style stepped amphitheatre designed by Pere Domènech i Roura with grandstands added for the 1992 Games.

PARKS

Parc de Joan Miró, Carrer d'Aragó, 2: 1989. Dominated by Miró's colourful sculpture clad in the broken tilework pioneered by Gaudí.

Parc de l'Espanya Industrial, Carrer de Muntadas, 37: 1985. A major architectural statement with towers surrounding a landscaped pool.

Parc de la Creueta del Coll, Passeig de la Mare de Déu del Coll, 77: 1987, MBM Architects/Martorell Bohigas Mackay. Landscaped pool garden in former quarry.

Parc del Centre del Poblenou, Av. Diagonal, 130: 2007, Jean Nouvel. Modern design with well planted shaded gardens.

Palau Reial de Pedralbes, Av. Diagonal, 686: 1920s. Royal palace, now a museum, in lovely gardens which are now a public park.

Parc del Laberint d'Horta, Passeig dels Castanyers: 18th century, Domenico Bagutti. Fabulous Baroque formal garden in upper town with pavilions, vistas and fountains.

BARCELONA HEIGHTS

Torre de Collserola, Ctra. de Vallvidrera al Tibidabo: 1992.,Norman Foster. Space-age telecommunications tower.

Sagrat Cor, Cumbre del Tibidabo: 1902–61, Enric Sagnier. Barcelona's answer to the church of the Cacre Coeur in Paris. Ornate Victoriana set on a vigorous Art Nouveau podium.

Fabra Observatory, Camí de l'Observatori: 1904, Josep Domènech i Estapà. Landmark on hills above the city.

Villa Almirall and Library, Cami de Vallvidrera al Tibidabo 42–45: 1924. Delightful fin de siècle pavilion architecture.

Villa Tibidabo, Camí de Vallvidrera al Tibidabo, 57: 1912, Albert Juan i Torner. Elegant ironwork.

Upper Station of the Vallvidrera funicular: 1905, Bonaventura Conill i Montobbio and Arnald Calvet i Peyronill. Characteristic cavernous entrance and Art Nouveau style.

Casa Arnús (Villa el Pinar), Carrer Manuel Arnús: 1904, Enric Sagnier. Built for a doctor ,Manuel Arnús i Fortuny.

UPPER TOWN

Santa Teresa de l'Infant Jesus, Via Augusta, 68: 1933, Josep Domènech i Mansana. Rugged masonry and giant arches in the manner of America's H H Richardson.

Santa Maria de Pedralbes Monastery, Baixada del Monestir, 9: 14th century. Set against a backdrop of hills with three tier cloister.

Former Hospital de la Santa Creu i Sant Pau, Carrer de Sant Quintí, 89: 1902–30, Lluís Domènech i Montaner. Never has a hospital had such consistently rich artistic and architectural treatment. The counterpart of Gaudí's Sagrada Familia.

La Rotonda, Passeig de Sant Gervasi, 51–53: 1906–11, Adolf Ruiz i Casamitjana. Conspicuous Art Nouveau design on a corner site. Look at contemporary houses on the road ascending the hill beside it.

CIVIC SPLENDOUR

University of Barcelona, Gran Via de les Corts Catalanes, 585: 1863–82, Elies Rogent. A monumental composition laid out around lovely courtyards with gardens behind. Impressive entrance hallway.

L'Escola Industrial, Carrer del Comte d'Urgell, 173–215: 1868. Industrial architecture in the Grand manner.

Hospital Clinic of Barcelona, Carrer de Villarroel, 170: 1906. Grandiose hospital in the Eixample with distinctive arch-topped portico.

Patronat Ribas College, Passeig Vall d'Hebron, 93–95: 1920–30, Enric Sagnier. Five gabled blocks originally built as an orphanage.

CosmoCaixa Science Museum, Carrer d'Isaac Newton, 26: 1909, Josep Domènech i Estapà. Trios of arches set in bold brick arches, originally built as an asylum for the blind.

Arenas de Barcelona, Gran Via de les Corts Catalanes, 373–85: 2011, Richard Rogers. Former bullring, constructed at the end of the 19th century, now roofed over and converted into a shopping centre with rooftop bars and restaurants.

La Monumental, Gran Via de les Corts Catalanes, 749: 1914, Domènec Sugrañes i Gras. Evocative former bullring, closed 2011, has much blue and white Mudéjar style tilework.

Artist's Acknowledgments

In 2007 I was involved in the preparation for a *Barcelona Sketchbook* with my late partner Rosamond Carter. Sadly she passed away in 2008, so her careful research was not used as the book was cancelled. So, in 2015, when Ian Pringle and Laurence King asked me to start again, a lot of her research was still valid — and I dedicate this book to her memory.

It has been a pleasure to team up again with my friend Marcus Binney, having worked with him on *Cambridge* and *London Sketchbooks*. His fantastic knowledge of Barcelona architecture has been an inspiration to me to paint and draw the city. I am grateful again to my editor Kim Inglis for her astute accuracy on the introduction and my handwritten notes. My designer Norreha Sayuti and production manager Janice Ng are a very talented team to work with. My thanks also go to my cousin Bonny Byfield for the use of her home and studio and to Jayne Norris for her perceptive support throughout the project.

Finally, I hope readers, whether they are residents or visitors, find Marcus Binney's descriptive writing and my watercolours a fitting tribute to the architecture of this amazing Catalan city.